Dwight D. Eisenhower

History Maker Bios

**Elaine Marie Alphin
and Arthur B. Alphin**

LERNER PUBLICATIONS COMPANY • MINNEAPOLIS

For all the soldiers and airmen who sallied forth across the Atlantic in the twentieth century to set Europe free and whose bodies now lie in the land they liberated.

—E. M. A. and A. B. A.

Illustrations by Tim Parlin

Text copyright © 2005 by Elaine Marie Alphin and Arthur B. Alphin
Illustrations copyright © 2005 by Lerner Publications Company

Lerner Publications Company
A division of Lerner Publishing Group
241 First Avenue North
Minneapolis, MN 55401 U.S.A.

Website address: www.lernerbooks.com

Library of Congress Cataloging-in-Publication-Data

Alphin, Elaine Marie.
 Dwight D. Eisenhower / Elaine Marie Alphin and Arthur B. Alphin.
  p.   cm. — (History maker bios)
 Includes bibliographical references and index.
 ISBN: 0–8225–1544–X (lib. bdg. : alk. paper)
  1. Eisenhower, Dwight D. (Dwight David), 1890–1969—Juvenile literature.
 2. Presidents—United States—Biography—Juvenile literature. [1. Eisenhower,
 Dwight D. (Dwight David), 1890–1969. 2. Presidents.] I. Alphin, Arthur B.
 II. Title. III. Series.
E836.A818 2005
973.921'092—dc22   200302647

Manufactured in the United States of America
1 2 3 4 5 6 – JR – 10 09 08 07 06 05

TABLE OF CONTENTS

INTRODUCTION

Dwight D. Eisenhower believed in fighting for what was right. As a boy, he fought with his fists. As a man, he led armies from nineteen different countries to win World War II.

Dwight knew how to lead a nation in peacetime too. As president, he stopped the Korean War. He built highways across the United States. He sent soldiers to protect black children entering an all-white school. He started a space program that would one day put Americans on the Moon.

Dwight Eisenhower served his country all his life.

This is his story.

1 BUT THAT'S NOT FAIR!

In 1900, when Dwight was ten, he wanted to go trick-or-treating with his big brothers. The Eisenhower boys did plenty of chores on their Kansas farm. Dwight knew he hoed vegetables and picked apples like his brothers. So he thought he should go out on Halloween with them too.

His father, David Eisenhower, said Dwight was too young. He couldn't stay out late with his teenage brothers, Edgar and Arthur.

Dwight thought that was unfair. He was so angry that he wanted to fight. He ran outside and hit an apple tree. He hit it as hard as he wanted to hit the rules that seemed so unfair.

Dwight was born in Denison, Texas. When he was a year old, the Eisenhowers moved to this house in Abilene, Kansas.

His father whipped him and sent him to his room. Dwight cried tears of rage. His mother, Ida, bandaged his hands. Then she told him, "He that conquers his own soul is greater than he that conquers a city."

Dwight never forgot his mother's words. He decided that it was all right to fight when he had to. But he should be careful not to get so angry that he couldn't think clearly. He shouldn't let his temper control him.

Dwight (LEFT) had five brothers. He was closest to Edgar, who stands to the right of Dwight.

Dwight (SECOND FROM LEFT IN FRONT ROW) in grade school

Dwight liked to read. In the evenings, his father read the Bible. Soon Dwight joined him. But Dwight really liked reading history books, especially books about ancient battles.

Dwight also loved playing baseball and football. He dreamed of playing professional ball. But when he was fourteen, he fell and cut his left knee. It swelled, and then his lower leg turned dark. That meant blood poisoning. The doctor wanted to cut off the leg to save Dwight's life.

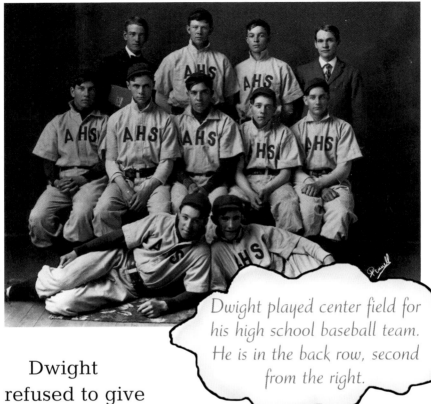

Dwight played center field for his high school baseball team. He is in the back row, second from the right.

Dwight refused to give up. He begged his brother Edgar not to let the doctor cut. He told Edgar, "I'd rather be dead than crippled and not be able to play ball."

Their parents trusted God to decide whether Dwight lived. For two days and nights, Edgar stood at Dwight's door, ready to stop the doctor. Finally, Dwight's body fought off the infection. His leg healed.

After Dwight got better, he spent long hours outdoors. He'd always wanted to go camping and hunting, but his father wasn't interested. Then Dwight met Bob Davis, an outdoorsman who wanted to share what he knew about fishing and hunting. Dwight learned everything he could.

Both Edgar and Dwight wanted to go to college. But their parents had no money. The brothers decided to pool their savings from work and take turns. Edgar was older, so he went first, entering the University of Michigan in 1909. Dwight worked at the local dairy, waiting his turn.

WHO'S IKE?

Ike was a nickname for Eisenhower. David and Ida called each of their boys Ike in turn. Dwight and Edgar were so close that their parents called Dwight "Little Ike" and Edgar "Big Ike." As Dwight grew up, the nickname stuck.

Cadets exercise at West Point.

Then Dwight heard about the U.S. Naval Academy at Annapolis, Maryland. He would have to pass hard tests to get in. But if he did, he wouldn't have to pay for his college education. Instead, he would serve as a naval officer. Annapolis even had a football team. Dwight decided to take the tests.

Although he passed them, another boy got better scores. That boy got the only available opening at the Naval Academy. But there was room at the U.S. Military Academy in West Point, New York. West Point students were called cadets. They served as army officers after finishing their education. Dwight decided to seek his future at West Point.

2 To Serve a Nation

On June 14, 1911, Dwight saw the granite walls of West Point for the first time. That evening, the twenty-year-old was sworn in as a cadet. Dwight hadn't thought about what it would mean to be a cadet and then an army officer. But when he took his cadet oath, he promised to do what his country wanted instead of what he wanted to do.

"The United States of America would now . . . mean something different than it ever had before," he wrote. "From here on, it would be the nation I would be serving, not myself."

Dwight played linebacker for the academy's football team. In November 1912, he hurt his right knee in a game. Later, he twisted it badly while riding a horse. The doctors managed to straighten the leg. But they said he could never play football again.

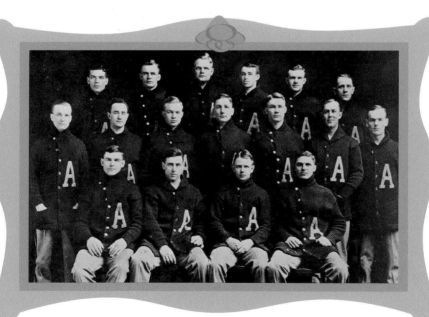

Dwight loved playing football for Army. He is third from left in the second row in this team photo.

Dwight became bitterly depressed. Then an officer asked him to coach the first-year football players. Dwight liked training the younger men. The officers saw that he had a talent for leadership and command.

Leadership and command were important in an officer, but so was good health. The doctors worried about Dwight's leg. They suggested that Dwight take an easy job when he graduated. But Dwight refused. When he graduated in 1915, he chose to be an infantry officer. In wartime, the infantry would do most of the fighting.

Dwight and Mamie met and fell in love after Dwight graduated from West Point.

Dwight went to Fort Sam Houston in Texas. He wanted to prove himself a good officer and overcome the worries about his leg. His hard work and devotion to duty impressed his commanding officers.

A friend introduced Dwight to Mamie Doud. Eighteen-year-old Mamie loved music and was lively and confident. Dwight fell in love with her. On Valentine's Day 1916, he asked her to marry him.

Mamie's parents weren't sure she should marry a soldier, but Mamie said yes. On July 1, 1916, Dwight was given a higher rank. He was promoted to First Lieutenant Eisenhower. He married Mamie the same day.

Only a month later, Dwight left for two weeks of training. Mamie couldn't believe he would leave her so soon. Dwight said, "My country comes first and always will. You come second." His honesty didn't kill their romance. Mamie understood her husband. She admired his dedication.

Dwight and Mamie got married on July 1, 1916.

In April 1917, the United States entered World War I. Dwight was promoted to captain. He immediately asked to go overseas to fight. Instead, he was sent to Georgia to train other soldiers. Mamie stayed in Texas, expecting the couple's first child.

Doud Dwight Eisenhower was born in September. He inherited the family nickname, Ike, but everyone called him Ikky. Dwight's life was full between family and training soldiers. But he wanted the chance to serve his country in combat himself.

Ike was sorry to be away when Ikky was born. He wrote to Mamie, "I've sent you 100,483,491,342 kisses since I've been gone."

3 A SOLDIER
BETWEEN WARS

In 1918, Dwight went to Pennsylvania to command a tank training center, where soldiers learned to operate tanks. He was fascinated by the new tanks and glad that Mamie and Ikky could join him. But he still wanted to fight in Europe.

On his twenty-eighth birthday, Dwight was promoted and ordered to go fight. But the war in Europe ended in November 1918—before he could get there.

Dwight was ashamed of not having fought, but even in peacetime, he could serve his country. In 1919, Dwight was assigned to try moving soldiers across the country by truck instead of the usual way, by train. He led a group of army trucks from Washington, D.C., to California.

In the early 1900s, cars and trucks were new to everyone—even the army.

In Maryland, Dwight again trained soldiers to use tanks.

Very few people owned a car or truck in the early 1900s. Roads were only dirt trails made for horse-drawn wagons. The trip was difficult. Dwight was shocked that the soldiers could travel only five miles an hour on some days.

Next, Dwight went to Camp Meade, Maryland. The Eisenhowers became popular with other military families. Everybody called Dwight by his family nickname, Ike. The men in Ike's command got Ikky a tank uniform. They took him with them on tank drills.

Ike and Colonel George S. Patton are circled in this picture. Ike is on the right.

Many of the officers at Camp Meade had served overseas in the Tank Corps. One was Colonel George S. Patton, who had fought in France. He and Ike spent hours discussing ways to use tanks in combat.

Then Ikky caught scarlet fever. The army doctors did everything they could, but in January 1920, he died. Both Ike and Mamie were heartbroken. Ike felt that losing his son was "the greatest disappointment and disaster of my life."

Ike buried his grief in his work. General Fox Conner saw good qualities in Ike and decided to help his career. The general invited Ike to his home and loaned Ike books about military planning and history. Then the men discussed how they could use the writers' ideas in future wars.

General Conner knew that the treaty that had ended World War I created many problems. It had taken land from Germany and given it to other countries. Germany was bitter and ready to fight again. As Ike and General Conner talked, Ike thought about leading soldiers in another war in Europe.

Ike and Mamie never forgot the son they lost. Ike sent Mamie flowers every year on Ikky's birthday.

The general also gave Ike special assignments where he could both learn and show his abilities. In 1922, General Conner took Ike to Panama as his aide. Mamie stayed home to have the Eisenhowers' second son, John. This boy was never called Ike. The family nickname died with Ikky.

After Panama, General Conner made sure Ike went to the Command and General Staff School. Only the army's best officers were accepted to the school. These officers were trained to lead the army in future wars. Ike graduated as the top student in his class in 1926. He was only thirty-five, younger than most of the other officers.

John wore his Boy Scout uniform on this trip to a park with Ike and Mamie in 1934.

In the 1930s, Ike served as the aide to some of the army's most important generals. He also worked on planning what the army would do if another war came.

Then, in September 1939, Germany invaded Poland. World War II began. This time, Ike wasn't the only Eisenhower determined to fight if the United States entered the war. John had grown into a young man. He told his father that he wanted to go to West Point and serve his country also.

ALWAYS AMERICA

From 1934 to 1938, Ike served in the Philippines with a group of U.S. military advisers. The Philippine president liked Ike so much that he offered to pay him anything to leave the army and stay in the Philippines. But Ike said, "No amount of money can make me change my mind. My entire life has been given to this one thing, my country."

4 SUPREME COMMAND

I ke was promoted again in 1941. His new job was to help General Walter Krueger plan war games. In these pretend battles, parts of the army fought each other the way they might fight enemies in Europe. War games tested battle plans and showed what worked and what didn't. Ike's war game ideas were outstanding, and General Krueger won.

The army was impressed with Ike's planning skills. They made him Brigadier General Eisenhower. Then, on December 7, 1941, the Japanese bombed Pearl Harbor in Hawaii. The United States entered World War II.

Within a week, Ike was ordered to Washington, D.C., to meet with General George C. Marshall. Ike's understanding of the war in Europe impressed General Marshall. But he had heard about Ike's temper. He tested Ike by warning him that he would probably spend the war sitting at a desk in Washington.

The United States entered World War II after the Japanese bombed Pearl Harbor in Hawaii on December 7, 1941.

German soldiers salute Adolf Hitler as he rides in a parade. Hitler convinced millions of Germans that their country should rule Europe.

After failing to fight in World War I, Ike wanted nothing more than to fight this time. But he had learned to control his temper. "I am trying to do my duty," he said. "If that locks me to a desk for the rest of the war . . . so be it!" Satisfied, General Marshall decided to promote Ike.

Ike suggested a bold plan for the Allies— the United States, Great Britain, and other countries that had joined forces to fight Germany and Japan. Ike wanted the Allies to attack by going through France into Germany. By this time, the Germans had taken over France. Ike planned to sweep into Germany and win complete victory.

General Marshall liked Ike's plan. He hoped to attack in 1943. He sent Ike to Great Britain in 1942 to explain the idea. The British didn't think they could be ready in time. But Prime Minister Winston Churchill liked Ike's thinking. He told Marshall that Ike should be given command of the U.S. forces in Europe.

Marshall agreed. He promoted Ike to major general and put him in charge of the other American generals and their soldiers.

Ike relaxed during his time off at Telegraph Cottage in England during World War II.

Ike planned and commanded the Allied invasion of North Africa in 1942. In 1943, he commanded the invasion of the island of Sicily, part of Italy. At last, he was serving his country in battle!

In December 1943, President Franklin D. Roosevelt and Prime Minister Churchill named Ike supreme allied commander. That gave Ike command of armies from nineteen different countries.

Ike (LEFT) as the commander of Allied forces in Africa. He stands with Henri-Honoré Giraud, a French general helping the Allies.

Ike shares a chat with a soldier in Europe during World War II.

Ike wanted to use his plan to attack Germany. But even though his rank gave him authority over generals from many Allied countries, each general wanted to do things his own way. Ike knew he must make the generals believe his idea was best. He spent long hours telling them how his plan would work. He refused to give up until they understood and agreed.

Ike wasn't able to visit his family often. Mamie missed him, although she understood that he had to be away. But when John came to Europe in 1944, she begged Ike to give John a safe desk job.

Ike refused. It was the one time Ike and Mamie seriously argued. But both Ike and John knew John's duty lay in combat. Ike would not spare his own son.

Ike's patience with the other generals paid off. He organized their troops to invade France and attack the German troops there. He chose June 6, 1944, for the invasion, called Operation Overlord. Although many Allied soldiers died, the Allies broke through the German defenses.

Dwight speaks to soldiers right before the attack on June 6, 1944, also known as D-Day.

War was even harder in snowy weather. Here U.S. soldiers dressed in their winter gear stand in line for a meal.

Ike's old friend, General George Patton, charged his tanks after the retreating German army. But as months passed, the attack slowed in the ice and snow of winter. Ike called "upon every man of all the Allies to rise to new heights of courage . . . and of effort."

The Allies attacked Germany from the west. At the same time, soldiers from the Soviet Union attacked Germany from the east. On May 7, 1945, Germany's leaders surrendered.

Ike had heard stories about the concentration camps run by Hitler's followers, the Nazis. In these terrible places, Nazis killed millions of Jews and members of other groups that the Nazis hated. When Ike finally saw the camps, they outraged him. The men, women, and children who had survived looked like walking skeletons. Ike brought in reporters and political leaders to expose the horrors to the world.

SUPREME RESPONSIBILITY

Ike knew that Operation Overlord might fail. He wrote a speech that he planned to give if the Allies were beaten back. "The troops, the air and the navy did all that bravery and devotion to duty could do. If any blame or fault attaches to the attempt, it is mine alone." Ike was the supreme commander. He would have taken complete responsibility for failure.

Ike also saw many Germans escaping to the West as soldiers from the Soviet Union marched across Germany. The Soviets wanted to force their form of government on Germany. This type of government was called communism. Soviet soldiers killed Germans who resisted. They also forced German scientists to come to the Soviet Union. Ike ordered his soldiers to help Germans escape to the West, and to offer freedom to any scientist who wanted to come to the United States.

In December, Ike was made the army chief of staff—the top general in command of the U.S. Army's troops around the world.

5 I LIKE IKE!

I ke retired from the army and became president of New York's Columbia University in 1948. But Soviet troops were still forcing Communism on Eastern Europe. The United States and many Western European nations created the North Atlantic Treaty Organization (NATO). These countries wanted to keep the peace. But they were determined to stop the Soviets, even if it meant going to war again.

In 1950, Communist North Korea invaded South Korea. U.S. troops went to Korea to fight the Communists. Ike itched to serve his country again.

When President Truman asked Ike to become supreme commander of NATO in 1951, he accepted. He helped Western European countries recover from the war and stopped the Soviets from moving into other countries. He also convinced Congress to send troops and supplies to support NATO.

This is the flag of the North American Treaty Organization (NATO). NATO was formed in 1949 to oppose communism.

Supporters from many states cheer for Ike to run for president in 1952.

Politicians suggested that Ike run for president. Ike wondered if he could serve his country better in the White House. He announced that he would lead "a crusade for freedom in America and freedom in the world." Voters were overjoyed. Cheers of "I like Ike!" greeted him everywhere. Ike was sixty-two when he was elected president of the United States in 1952.

President Eisenhower used the same methods in the White House that General Eisenhower had used in the army. He chose good people who knew their jobs and put them in charge of different departments. Then he led them all in working toward a common goal.

One of Ike's first goals was to deal with the Korean War. He visited Korea and studied battle plans. He decided that the United States couldn't win this war. So he made peace and brought the troops home.

President Eisenhower visits troops in the Korean War.

Some generals wanted to fight in Vietnam in 1954 to stop the Communists there. Ike listened. But he decided this was another war that would risk too many American lives for too little gain. He refused.

However, Ike wanted Americans to be safe in the future. If they did have to fight another war, he wanted to hold the high ground: outer space.

Ike hoped that Americans would one day reach the Moon. Years later, in 1969, astronauts met that goal.

Ike's highway system created new roads like this one in South Carolina.

Ike told the air force to work on space research. The German scientists who had come to the United States after World War II helped. In 1958, Ike created the National Aeronautics Space Administration (NASA) to make sure Americans would take the lead in exploring space.

Ike wanted to improve things at home too. He remembered traveling by truck in 1919. He wanted to build a system of highways across the United States to make travel easier. Some state governments didn't like the idea. But the system wouldn't work without all the states. Ike made sure the states got the task done.

In two terms as president of the United States, Ike worked hard to give the American people a peaceful time after a hard-fought war. He built the future instead of fighting the battles of the past. And he continued to serve his country with honor.

Ike retired in 1961. He'd suffered two heart attacks while he was president. As a private citizen, he tried to rest. He painted and wrote books. But he had more heart attacks.

IKE'S HOBBIES

Ike liked a good game of golf, but when it rained, he couldn't play. Then he found a hobby that he could enjoy in any weather—painting. His first painting was of Mamie. It turned out so strangely that it made people laugh. But Ike kept painting, and he got better. As president, he sent out holiday cards printed with his artwork.

Ike liked to paint copies of photographs. He tried to get every detail just right.

On March 28, 1969, Dwight D. Eisenhower died. He told Mamie that he loved her and his children and grandchildren. His last words were, "I have always loved my country."

The American people loved Ike in return. A train carried his body home to Kansas to be buried. Along the way, people wanted to say good-bye. So many people stood beside the train tracks to pay their respects that the train could not safely go faster than twenty-five miles an hour.

TIMELINE

In the year . . .

1911   Dwight became a cadet at the U.S. Military Academy at West Point, New York.

Age 20

1915   he graduated from West Point and entered the infantry.

1916   he married Mamie Doud.

1917   the United States entered World War I.
his son, Ikky, was born.

1920   Ikky died.

1922   he traveled to Panama.
his second son, John, was born.

1926   he graduated from the Command and General Staff School.

Age 35

1941   the United States entered World War II.

1942   he was placed in charge of U.S. forces in Europe.
he led an invasion of North Africa.

1943   he was named supreme allied commander.

1944   he led the invasion of France on D-Day, June 6.

Age 53

1945   Germany surrendered.
he was made army chief of staff.

1951   he became supreme commander of NATO.

1952   he was elected president of the United States

Age 62

1953   he ended fighting in the Korean War.

1956   he was reelected president.

1957   he ordered troops in Arkansas to help black children attend an all-white school.

1958   he created NASA.

1969   he died on March 28.

Age 78

FOR THE CHILDREN

In 1954, the highest court in the United States ruled that black children and white children must go to the same schools. Before the Supreme Court made this ruling, many black children went to separate schools. Those schools usually didn't offer a good education.

In 1957, nine black children tried to go to an all-white school in Little Rock, Arkansas. The state's governor ordered the Arkansas National Guard not to let the students enter the school. Armed soldiers barred them from the doors.

Ike was outraged that a state governor had refused to obey the Supreme Court. Even worse, the governor had ordered soldiers to disobey the court too. Ike sent troops to take the children safely into school.

People march in the South in the 1950s. They are protesting separate schools for black children and white children.

FURTHER READING

Lucas, Eileen. *Cracking the Wall: The Struggles of the Little Rock Nine.* Minneapolis: Carolrhoda Books, Inc., 1997. This illustrated book tells the story of the nine African American children who struggled to attend an all-white school in Little Rock, Arkansas, and how Ike helped them succeed.

Stein, R. Conrad. *D-Day.* Danbury, CT: Children's Press, 1993. This book presents the details of Ike's invasion of France on June 6, 1944, also known as D-Day.

Whitman, Sylvia. *Children of the World War II Home Front.* Minneapolis: Carolrhoda Books, Inc., 2001. Learn about the lives of children who waited at home while family members fought under Ike's leadership in World War II.

Young, Jeff C. *The Korean War.* Berkeley Heights, NJ: Enslow Publishers, Inc., 2003. From battles to weapons, this book describes the war that Ike decided the United States should stop fighting.

WEBSITES

***American Experience:* Dwight D. Eisenhower**
<http://www.pbs.org/wgbh/amex/presidents/34 _eisenhower/> This website for the PBS television show *American Experience* includes a biography, timeline, and fun facts about Ike.

The Dwight D. Eisenhower Library
<http://www.eisenhower.utexas.edu> This library preserves papers and letters written by Ike. On the website, you can see Ike's signature, family and military photographs, and examples of Ike's paintings.

The White House: Dwight D. Eisenhower
<http://www.whitehouse.gov/history/presidents/de34.html>
The White House presents the story of Ike's life. This website includes a link to a biography of Mamie Doud Eisenhower.

SELECT BIBLIOGRAPHY

Davis, Kenneth S. *Soldier of Democracy: A Biography of Dwight Eisenhower.* Garden City, NY: Doubleday, Doran, 1945.

Eisenhower, Dwight D. *At Ease: Stories I Tell to Friends.* Garden City, NY: Doubleday, 1967.

Eisenhower, Dwight D. *The Papers of Dwight David Eisenhower.* Ed. Alfred D. Chandler Jr. Baltimore: Johns Hopkins Press, 1970.

Eisenhower, John S. D. *General Ike: A Personal Reminiscence.* New York: The Free Press, 2003.

Ferrell, Robert H., ed. *The Eisenhower Diaries.* New York: W. W. Norton, 1981.

Holland, Matthew F. *Eisenhower between the Wars.* Westport, CT: Praeger, 2001.

Kinnard, Douglas. *Eisenhower: Soldier-Statesman of the American Century.* Washington, D.C.: Brassey's, 2002.

Miller, Merle. *Ike the Soldier.* New York: Putnam's Sons, 1987.

Pach, Chester J., and Elmo Richardson. *The Presidency of Dwight D. Eisenhower.* Lawrence: University Press of Kansas, 1991.

Perret, Geoffrey. *Eisenhower.* New York: Random House, 1999.

INDEX

Acknowledgments

For photographs and artwork: Dwight D. Eisenhower Library, pp. 4, 7, 8, 10, 14, 16, 17, 18, 21, 22, 24, 29, 31, 43; © CORBIS, p. 9; United States Military Academy Library, p. 12; Wernher Krutein/photovault.com, p. 20; © Todd Strand/Independent Picture Service, p. 23; Library of Congress, pp. 27, 30; *Illustrated London News*, p. 28; National Archives, pp. 32, 33, 39; NATO Photo, p. 37; Southdale Hennepin County Library, p. 38; NASA, p. 40; American Automobile Association Manufacturers Association, p. 41; © Bettmann/CORBIS, p. 45; Front cover: Dwight D. Eisenhower Library. Back cover: National Museum of American History, Smithsonian Institution. **For quoted material:** pp. 8, 10, 22, 28, 33, Eisenhower, Dwight D. *At Ease*. Garden City, NY: Doubleday, 1967; pp. 14, 25, 38, Eisenhower, Dwight D. *In Review: Pictures I've Kept, a Concise Pictorial Autobiography*. Garden City, NY: Doubleday, 1969; pp. 17, 34, Perret, Geoffrey. *Eisenhower*. New York: Random House, 1999; p. 18, D'Este, Carlo. *Eisenhower*. New York: Henry Holt, 2002; p. 43, Eisenhower, Susan. *Mrs. Ike: Memories and Reflections on the Life of Mamie Eisenower*. New York: Farrar, Straus & Giroux, 1996.